sitting with the darkness

A Collection of Thoughts
ANNABELLE CHAPMAN

Annabelle Chapman
PO Box 4148
Springfield Central QLD 4300

Instagram: dragonfly.wing.dreams
Website: www.annabellechapman.com

sitting with the darkness

for my darling cat, Leila.

sitting with the darkness

PROLOGUE

there are times, when it is darkest, you will have to be your own rescue. you will have to love yourself and want better. teach yourself better. you will need to wake up tomorrow, and try again. you will have to look yourself in the mirror and forgive yourself for all of your failings, because sometimes, it is only your own forgiveness that you truly need.

always be kind, and show more kindness. even when it does not feel deserved or warranted. particularly, for yourself.

DEPTH

❖

"for all the words i have, & the thousand of ways i can string them together, i still feel continuously misunderstood"

& if my heart is breaking,
let it break
i can feel my sadness -
like a weight on my chest,
it is all that i can carry.
to think and overthink -
it adds. & it adds.
slowly tearing me down

sitting with the darkness

my thoughts go deeper than tree roots,
& entwine themselves around my very nervous system -
until over time,
they constrict, consume, & control the flow -
little glimmers of sunlight touching the new leaves to feed the strength
i almost need a tidal wave, to crash right through me,
& wipe it clear
to give my lungs oxygen, so i can breathe -
the silence is so loud. deafening and lonely.
it is the perfect soil for roots to grow

how sad, yet heavy with accuracy
i think of you all the time,
but you don't think of me at all
              — — — — —
            would i want you to?
            with a heart like a yo-yo on a trampoline
            i'm not even sure you know which way is up
            even when you're looking at the sky

sitting with the darkness

at this table, there is room for more
but you eat for one
leaving nothing but crumbs.

my heart is hurting.
but it was me.
i lit the fire,
& i gave it fuel

sitting with the darkness

i am burning in this love.
chains tangled
& locked around my feet -
yet,
i could reach for the key
but i won't look.
i choose not to see.
there is a transaction that must be made,
a simple,
yet,
heavy exchange,
to set myself free from this self-made prison,
& find my way to the clearing -
but -
i dare not pay the price,
for,
i must tear out my heart
to let go of my vice.
instead -
i would rather drown in this unrequited love,
letting go of my sense,
my sanity
& myself.

sitting with the darkness

i am a recluse with my nostalgic nonsense,
recalling rose-tinted memories,
that simply,
never were.

i feel my empty cup.
i see it, and i hear it.
it is being filled.
i open my mouth to drink it,
but i cannot taste it.
nothing is there.
only air.

i walk a desert road,
then complain no one is there to help me carry the load

sitting with the darkness

i have found i live my life with a measuring device
of 'this is okay' and 'i can live with this'
but so little makes it to that,
that i am so terrified to look to the sky.
who will reach me if i am so high?
don't look!
i left the picket fence i had built around my baseline
so acclimatised to the comfort,
i fell asleep.
wake up!
i think i looked only once before i jumped.
free falling into the abyss,
i did not think to miss it all.
i found more comfort in the fall

i miss them.
they were so hurtful, but
i miss them.
i miss the company in my own destruction
— — — — —

these memories burn & stain everything they touch.
what a fool i have been.
there is too much pain in today,
i should sleep.

like acid rain,
she's burning you black.
slowly smoking,
smouldering -
turning everything to ash.
her black ocean,
all for you

— — — — —

i cannot see our way clear
your chain is heavy & i cannot break it
i feel alone in this darkness,
yet -
heavy even with my own chain,
i would take two

— — — — —

my oars have not moved
nor my boat altered course -
ash laps at the sides.
your anchor was always mine

the walls are black,
cold,
& rotten -
rooms filled with endless mirrors,
& deceit -
your hands now worn,
empty,
& bare.
a prizeless effort to stay in her stead

sitting with the darkness

am i crazy?
i have been so alone with my thoughts
i have fallen in love with their lullabies
slowly drifting and sifting the sadness
deep into my mind

from the faintest whisper of an idea
you form the most beautiful palette,
brushing with every colour ever imagined -
& with it, you paint a full scene.
metres upon metres,
from a thought, you have distorted reality
& blurred the lines between that & your dreams -
and then you cry.
you cry when the illusion is shattered.
every.
single.
time.

forgive me.
my imagination is running away with itself.
i would shoot it with my gun,
if only it were loaded

the shortness in my breath
stings in my heart -
i still feel it all.
never a blessing -
always a curse.

i wanted it so badly,
to inhale into something real & fit into your square.
but i knew -
i know it now in my heart,
i don't belong there.
like a thin coat of black paint over white,
something within me was cracking through.
but in my effort to deny myself the lie,
i've scarred my heart with the memories of good times,
so few, but so deep.
even still it weighs on me.
and it aches.

& in the beginning,
i felt fireworks & bursts of stardust in my heart.
but how -
when?
now it is all black,
& i am wading through tar,
fighting for my life in this deep sadness.

i am not brave,
for i do not open my eyes to see the magnitude of the being
when i creak the door to the feed the beast

i will fill my pockets with stones,
& let the water meet my lungs.
— — — — —

this love feels like a facade

i want to believe we have no rules
but these rules are the ones my dreams have placed on me

i cannot eat,
for these memories they sit,
in the very pit of my stomach,
churning my soul

sitting with the darkness

SHIFTING

❖

"& you would think, for all the flowers and butterflies, my thoughts and words would be prettier than they are"

so fickle with your love,
high up in your fortress
you cannot feel the falling blossoms on your face
when you shield yourself so well with mirrored armour

your indifference has become contagious
a heart so impartial
the map morphs & changes from sunrise to sunset
& i have been dancing blissfully in my ignorance
skipping out of time -
but the winds' whispers have become loud
and now that the haziness has cleared from my eyes
i find,
i am lost in these woods
with a map that makes no sense,
to a key that isn't mine.

i am struggling to let you go -
the crevices of my heart are clinging to the dream of us
like an overgrown vine

sitting with the darkness

i cannot stomach this.
i am choked up & cannot cry out.
like rocks in my lungs,
i am struggling to breathe,
i am struggling to believe -
something in this is tying knots in my stomach
that will not be undone.

& all i can do,
is sit here,
internally inconsolable
with thoughts,
of how your heart is no longer mine

i don't really like what this love makes of me.
i am jealous, recluse & envious.
i am a fool.
i am desperate for your rationed time & affection.
my cup waves between half empty & half full.
i have become a beggar for a fullness
that you will never give me.
& in moments of deep doubt,
i have glimmers of rationality -
that i should take it upon myself to unlove you,
to remove my tight stitches
that i have sewn to the dream that i always feel is my next course,
my next day,
the next page -
but,
these moments of clarity are short lived.
my determination and belligerence are slowly killing me.
i will not let myself see my way clear.
i have gone mad on this half love.

whilst i have been madly in love with him,
i have lost myself.

sitting with the darkness

i am fractured,
i am flawed.
i want to cut these shackles free.
these shackles and chains of a long,
constant,
line of errors in judgement
& of poor decisions,
all linking me to this moment.
how i have strayed so far,
collecting my shitty decisions
& intertwining the compounding consequences
like rotten daisy chains

my frail & nimble fingers reach for the phone
it's winter -
but there are no blankets
or fire
that can warm me in this cold
— — — — —

you answer my call.
i choke.
this phone cord has wound its way around my neck
forming a noose for my throat

dawn is on the horizon,
flowers are in bloom,
encouraging me to move,
yet -
still -
my heart is empty
like there's someone missing,
that i never knew at all.

i have broken & resewn my heart together
in an effort just to be with you.
but now,
my needle is broken,
& my thread is out -
& you look to me,
feeling cheated in your own defeat,
like i am to blame.

i sat in the winter sun,
with the grass under my feet,
i watched the ants work beneath the grass leaves -
& though my mind was empty,
my heart was still heavy.

i cannot make sense,
when my head & my heart,
they do not speak the same

sitting with the darkness

i am smoking too much,
& thinking of you.

i am a well of mistakes,
regrets & awful decisions.
but what can i do?
i cannot convince myself that,
despite my poorly state,
i too, deserve love.

sitting with the darkness

it is a heavy burden,
to feel so much & yet,
express so little -
— — — — —
my handcuffs are my silence.
they are all that holds me here in this in-between.
caught here,
torn -
 between staying the same,
and letting go.

i crave the love of a woman
deep within my soul.
i crave for a bond i've never known.

sitting with the darkness

i am not looking for anyone to utter my name,
only the long,
undemanding,
silence.

the time we shared together,
will always be in my heart,
but now it has passed -
& it is time for me to let you go

sitting with the darkness

FRACTURED

❖

"i am not who i once was, & yet, i will never be this person again"

i am not yet ready,
    to confront the part of me that is missing.

did i take for granted everything i had with you?
this is the question that burns my very soul,
when all else has been eaten away

i sat in agony with my feelings,
until they all blurred together
& i could not name them
they blended and they moulded
an anchor around my heart -
i became so breathless,
starving for air -
yet i could not break away.
i had to pull myself apart.

i cannot correct my thoughts
i cannot break free to live how i desire
and thereby,
i make my own prison

how can i love so deeply
that which pierces,
& tears apart,
the very veins in my being

sitting with the darkness

i wanted with every fibre of my being for this to be it. for us to be right. i struggle with the idea that i couldn't do enough to make this work. i bent. i moulded. but i could not make myself fit. i couldn't forgo all i ever wanted just to be with you, when you place me last at every turn. in times i needed you most, it was always just below enough. like a half-starved child, i held out my hands for crumbs and tried to glue them together and called it love. because to me it was love. i loved you. i love you. but i cannot live a life on a piece meal diet of affection. when i am so starved and i am pouring all i have out, how can i ever have anything, for anyone, or even, myself.

i look to the bed where you once slept,
and all i can feel is an aching sadness.
i am so melancholic since you left.
you left. tearing yourself from our interwoven cloth.
and i am here,
jagged and raggedy, with my threads all coming apart.
i have no skills to fix the space that you have made.
& in such a fast fashion, you ripped yourself away.
oh, what a mess.
thread by thread.
year by year.
i am coming undone.

a mirror does not lay bare a reflection for me,
for i do not know who i am anymore.
i am dissociating and daydreaming.

& then i apologise,
tormenting myself with my mistakes

sitting with the darkness

he is breaking apart the very fabric of my bones,
without lifting a finger at all

you ask for a pool,
but i am only capable of an ocean

sitting with the darkness

i love you endlessly,
but you cannot come near me.

i look at this picture,
and all i remember,
is being utterly and entirely in love with you.
these images play memory reels in my head,
& every single one is played
with every colour of the universe -
it is so captivating.
almost as if,
until now,
my life would only ever playback in greyscale.
— — — — —
& i wonder,
if you can place your finger
exactly on the moment,
where you knew
you would never feel that way about me at all

i wanted him to hurt,
like how he'd hurt me.
i was thinking of all the things i could say,
hurtful but true.
i wanted him to feel guilty,
to feel horrendously ashamed,
of how he'd been -
but,
instead of my words,
i just choked on my silence.

i have wandered for years,
with this worn old compass,
& countless,
now tired,
maps.
but still.
for all my wandering,
still -
i have no sense of direction into your heart

in the coldness of your shadow,
i admire the beauty of your cracked halo

i am in love,
but you are only visiting

HAUNTED

❖

"nicotine, caffeine, & these dreams"

a devotion that transcends this realm,
& the next

i am too tired
& too worn,
to begin to utter
the heaviness my heart bears

i love to replay this song,
over
& over
& over again.
it's the closest i ever feel,
to the ghost of you

sitting with the darkness

i am as full,
as i am empty and confused.
how can you dream your future with me,
& then leave me alone in this cold?

you left -
tearing not,
but leaving a small,
pin size hole,
in the bottom of my heart -
& slowly it drips,
pouring out my love,
into the pit of my being.
it does not belong there.
but,
what can i do?
i cannot find the hole.
i cannot begin to mend.

sitting with the darkness

i wouldn't wish for you to have to continue in this hell,
but can you just give me ten more minutes,
& explain to me again,
why you had to go?

my soul knows yours.
it has known you all along.

— — — — —

one day when we meet again,
i will tell you then,
as i would tell you now -
you were never alone.

sitting with the darkness

my own house
doesn't feel like home.
each corner hides my shame,
holds my sorrow,
& cradles my pain.

i cannot stop loving you.
lord knows, i have tried.
i have tried -
but,
the heavy steel door to my heart is closed & locked,
& you alone
are with me there.

sitting with the darkness

i am so small.
this guilt is lacing its way around my lungs.
it will not be undone.

— — — — —

       i am not the master of my time.
       this regret & pain is pinpricking my fingertips,
       drawing me down,
       holding me here.
       there is no escape.

the wound cannot begin to heal,
for i won't cut myself from you

sitting with the darkness

murmurs & whispers.
conversations with the ghost of you

i sit with your memory,
as if you were still here.

— — — — —

watching tv,
& i feel you there,
just as i drift off to sleep

MOONLIGHT

❖

"such love in the warmth of your hand"

city lights & empty streets -
sneaking kisses at crossings -
if i could live forever in any moment,
it would be any memory with you.

her hair is soft,
her voice kind,
& i am staring at her in awe.

you are within me,
& i, you -
show me a universe where we stay together
& take me there.

your hand in mine,
& i am dreaming of galaxies

it's so simple here.
loving you & ordering food.

gently,
suddenly.
& impatiently fast
— — — — —
"lucky," you say,
knowing,
i had no choice.
like i would even,
or ever
wanted a choice at all

she kissed me
& ignited a revolution in my heart.
i could move mountains,
i could walk this earth for an age,
& never find another
who can touch the light in my soul
& bring it forth like a new sunrise,
with just her lips

i am too happy in this moment.
the floor is crumbling beneath my feet.
i am free falling,
but all i can think is how
i would trace all the lengths of every world & universe
just to have our time together again

i am captivated by all that you are.

sitting with the darkness

i feel eyes on us,
& i hope they see -
how insanely,
irrevocably,
& endlessly,
i am in love with you

please stay.
i think i would like to kiss you one more time before you go,
and venture home.

i am here.
i have arrived.
& in so,
i have begun my slow soft fall

warm gentle wind.
grey overcast sky.
sunday street quiet.
our fingers intertwined.
— — — — —

i am so blessed to have had this moment in my lifetime.

sitting with the darkness

your hand behind your head,
i trace my fingers from your neck,
to where your collarbone meets your chest.
i am enraptured.

if i am calm,
and remain ever so still,
perhaps,
he will see the safety in my heart

sitting with the darkness

i am reliving and taking up my home
in the memories of our moments.
the wind shakes at my door, whispering doubt and anxiety,
that maybe this isn't for me -
but i turn the music louder and reinforce the locks.
i am a fool for you.

cold grass. warm air. blue neon lights.
sparsely scattered stars in the night sky.
your face is but centimetres from mine.
& in this moment,
i am ever so in love with being alive.

my roots are deepening,
and i do not care to stop them.

fold into me & let me care for your soul

sitting with the darkness

i lay on you so comfortably,
fitting so perfectly,
listening to your heartbeat & slowly drifting off to sleep,
as if it were playing for only me.

do you believe in love at first sight?
i believe in differing levels of love -
the way you can taste ice cream for the first time
and instantly love it -
or a dear friend you've had for a long time & care for deeply.
surely then,
love is like a tree.
branches upon branches,
differing heights and lengths,
new leaves and old,
with some that die and some that thrive.
surely then,
if this is so,
you could begin to love someone the moment you meet them,
& then from that,
it just continues to grow

a love that transcends all sense & reasonability.
a love that burns,
& sets my soul on fire

endlessly entwined in the thought of you & i

sitting with the darkness

please,
invite me into your heart,
so that i can build a home
with a warm fire hearth.
i would like to sleep there,
and stay a while
or forever -
if you like

the softness of your lips,
so quick and lightly
touch my hand.
my words escape me.
& i smile,
helplessly.

— — — — —

it is not a firework,
nor a raging flame -
but the lightness of a soft butterfly,
slowly lifting my heart

my heart is begging to be yours.
won't you let it?

i cup his face in my hand as he closes his eyes,
letting the weight of all he carries,
slowly,
but gently,
sit in the palm of my hand

there is a milky way of scattered stardust in my atmosphere,
ever since we kissed

as you lay bare your soul to me,
i feel as if,
i am touching the very inner light of the stars themselves

sitting with the darkness

no-one is perfect,
yet,
naively,
i still believe -
that the depths of his enigma heart
were made for only me.

maybe we can start again,
old love like new love -
adore each other intimately,
& kiss each other like it's the first time

REFLECTION

❖

"my heart is too good for someone who only wants to be half mine"

why would you let me love you,
when you were yet to make up your mind?

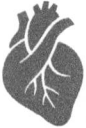

i cannot begin to heal myself,
with your hands firmly around my neck

i am struggling to learn to confront
the most vulnerable & damaged parts of me.
to sit with the pain,
to hear it awake
& with a voice,
to understand its reason & purpose -
— — — — —
too often I allow my fear to soothe it,
& lull it back to sleep.

sitting with the darkness

i would have loved you
forever,
if you had only let me -
but holding me at arms length,
leaving me hungry,
empty -
has now left you lonely.

please don't swallow me whole in your big dreams.
i have just come up for air -
i need to breathe.

sitting with the darkness

my shattered soul is only,
& all
my own.

is this your way of bringing me to you?
to dangle the warm sunlight
on a spiderweb thread

sitting with the darkness

i am not yet ready
to plunge completely,
wholly,
deep in this pool of love with you -
can i dip my toes for a while?
can i watch you & wait for the sun to be just right?

— — — — —

i need to mourn the loss of moonlight -
the hour is early,
i am cold,
& i am tired.

i am an endless quilt for mending.
& all the secrets i have so tightly wound into each stitch,
will dissolve your artwork image of me.
it is only a matter of time.
you have begun examining the detail in the fraying fabric.
it is only a matter of time.

sitting with the darkness

i won't bleed to soothe your sorrow

i feel the cyclone of pain inside me,
& use this energy,
to set myself free.

sitting with the darkness

i am tired,
& simply want be loved.

please let me sleep,
so i can dream -
dream a life without these memories
— — — — —
i have tried to love you,
with palms wide open
holding my breath,
silencing my heart -
but this is enough.
i have had enough.
let me go,
i beg of you -
loosen your newly tightened grip around my heart,
& let me be

i can almost taste the sweetness of these shackles
sinking without me,
while i rise above

is this me?
like an odd shape to a circular hole,
i cannot bring my edges in.
i strive & try to fit myself through.
& yet,
i am dying to do more of what separates me from you.
build myself up in a tower so high,
that no one could reach me if they tried.

sitting with the darkness

this cannot be all that there is.
there must be more,
somewhere out there in the wide expanse
of fresh air,
starry nights & green life.
there must be.

you are making your future plans
with a version of me that is yet to be
— — — — —
do not hold me on your pedestal.
i am far from the image you have of me.
i am bruised,
i am torn,
frayed at my edges,
i have been re-glued and re-sewed,
over & over -
i make no sense.
i am a mismatched pattern of pain.
but-
maybe,
if you see this all,
& still,
even still -
please instead,
place me on the bottom stair,
& let me make my way there -
i have not earned this love.
i am undeserving of your unconditional adoration.
please,
let me come to you,
crawl & climb my way to you,
one step at a time,
till i stand before you
& slowly,
piece by piece,
become bare -
showing you my heart,
& all that i keep there.

sitting with the darkness

HISTORY

Bittersweet nothing

Dancing to the sweet sound of silence
Kissing the bitter taste of nothing
Hugging the emptiness that lingers inside
Loving the hollow shadow that dwells in the dark

All what it means to feel at ease
All what is needed to let it go
Let all of it go
Let you go

Memories sing softly in the background
Treading lightly on the grass
The morning dew leaves a scent
As if the world was never at war

All what it means to feel alone
All what is needed to be with something
With someone
Other than you

sitting with the darkness